Òwe

Yoruba in Proverbs

A. A. Kila

Akada Press

Akada Press
MBC Unit 24 Millmead Road London N17 9QU
www.akadapress.com

First published in 2003

British Library Cataloguing in Publication Data
Data available

ISBN 0-9545465-0-4
Illustrations by Reggie Pedro & Ben Adedipe
Cover Design by Adam Williams

CONTENTS

PREFACE

In my quest for the means to understand different cultures and societies and the factors which regulate and determine their ways of life, I have always been fascinated by the capacity of proverbs to encapsulate complex themes and ideas.

The proverbs cited in the following pages were initially collected for my personal studies. I realised, however, that not only did they succinctly express some Yoruba concepts but they also helped to illumine the society in which they originated. This has, above all, motivated me to share them with others who may be interested. The selection of Yoruba proverbs presented in this book is intended to provide the reader with a glimpse into the culture of the Yoruba people. Only those proverbs which are both typical of Yoruba proverbs and easily understood by those unfamiliar with the Yoruba people and culture are included here.

Many people have contributed to the research and compilation of this book. Here I would like to remember and thank Adriana Piga the first person to suggest writing this book, Bola Ajayi and Fidel de Silva who helped with the gleanings of proverbs, Chief Adeola Adeyemi my main contact with oral sources, Cecilia Gatto Trocchi with whom I had long and lively discussions about some of the ideas expressed here, Danny Aeberhard who worked through the whole book, Valentina Buonumore, whose friendship laid a bridge between us and of course my own Francesca who was always there for me and to whom I say *avevi ragione c'e l'abbiamo fatta*.

A. A. Kila

FOREWORD

There are about 25 million people who recognize themselves as Yoruba people and they live mainly Nigeria and Benin (formerly the Kingdom of Dahomey). The Diaspora induced by centuries of slave trade and immigration have however taken their descendants and culture to countries like Gambia, Sierra Leone, Brazil, Cuba and to the eastern cities of the United States of America, to the UK and now to Ireland.

Since around AD 1000, the Yoruba people built a thriving network of cities and trading routes. Most of their cities and towns still exist today and many of the original societal structures are still intact. Their kings, known as Oba, are regarded as sacred, and they live in the town centres encircled by chiefs.

In the Yoruba world view, there is a supreme God called Olorun and about four hundred deities called *Orisha* who are his emissaries. The complexity of the Yoruba cosmology has led many western scholars to compare them to the pantheon of the ancient Greeks. In countries such as Brazil and Cuba where the Yoruba and their traditions have an impact on the social life, the rituals of the *Orisha* have been incorporated into Christian rituals to create a syncretistic religion called Santeria.

According to the myths, the world began at Ile-Ife, a city of great historical and religious significance in the heart of the Yoruba nation. This is where Olorun lowered a chain from the sky to allow a party of deities led by Oduduwa, the ancestor of mankind, to descend into the world. Before leaving the sky, the deities were given a cockerel, some earth, and a palm kernel. When Oduduwa got to the world it was covered with water. He threw the earth into the water and then lowered the cockerel onto it. The cockerel scratched it and the earth expanded to become land while the kernel grew into a tree with sixteen limbs; from this beginning, farmland spread across the world. Ile-Ife in fact literally means "the land expands".

The Yoruba people believe everything in life is related and that every aspect of life is a continuum. They believe that a person who dies does not cease to exist but goes to join the realm of the ancestors where he or she still has influence on the world. Maskers called *Egungun* are paraded to embody and pay homage to the deceased ancestors. The Yoruba consider every god and every religion as legitimate expressions representing the various routes available to conduct mankind to the same God and to allow human beings to accomplish their destiny. They believe that each one of us has to seek and follow the most appropriate god or religion for our personality and goals in life. Although it is believed that everybody has a chosen destiny before coming into the world, ultimately each person must take responsibility to develop the good character, *iwa*, necessary to fulfil their destiny.

In this book, which is part of the result of intense epistemological research in cultural anthropology, A. A. Kila uses Yoruba proverbs to give us a flavour of a complex and imposing culture. While he is very committed to African culture and values he is also keen on demystification. In his view it is not demystification that kills a tradition but ignorance. When choosing the proverbs presented in the following pages he was careful to avoid romanticizing the Yoruba people nor to attribute to them any bizarre qualities.

In that the human topics covered are resonant and familiar and the analysis original and illuminating, in my view, *Òwe – Yoruba Proverbs* may be compared to Erasmus of Rotterdam's *Adagio* and A. Arthaber's *Dizionario Comparato*. When I read the final draft, I found the contents fascinating and provocative. Accessible to all readers, it will certainly prompt their interest in Yoruba culture. While the imagery of the proverbs is located in the particulars of the Yoruba culture, the analysis conveys the universality of human nature.

Fidel de Silva
Rio de Janeiro

COLLABORATION

Àjèjé owo kan ko gbe igbá de ori.

No single hand, regardless of its might, can lift and place a calabash on the head.

Amongst the Yoruba, it is a very common practice for people to carry loads on their heads. In traditional society, the calabash in all its different forms and sizes is one of the most frequently-used containers for drinks and the usual vessel in which palm wine is kept, and from which it is served and sold.

The status of the calabash in Yoruba society has changed through time. In recent years, the growing trend in rural areas and villages has been to replace it with various types of aluminium, metal and plastic containers. In those areas where it still survives in daily use, the calabash continues to be a simple and practical container. By contrast, its presence in the cities is slowly but noticeably increasing. Here calabashes have become appreciated both for their aesthetic qualities and as symbols of tradition and are now mainly used as decorative articles for homes and in public buildings.

The Palm Wine Drinkers' Club, comprised mainly of university students, uses the calabash as one of its main symbols. The students, wishing to revive and exalt their traditional culture, strive to create a comradely spirit and, in their ever-festive reunions, use colourful expressions, sing folk songs and drink palm wine.

This proverb draws upon the fact that, the unwieldy form of the calabash makes it inherently difficult to handle. Like all bowls, once filled it is impossible to lift or manoeuvre with just one hand. The saying reminds us that there are certain situations and tasks which are meant to be tackled with the help of others, never alone. The proverb is often used to exhort someone guilty of not doing so to confide in or to share responsibilities with a partner, friend, sibling or member of the community.

Ówó omode ko to pepe,
Ti agbalagba ko wo akèrégbè.

The hand of a child cannot reach the shelf,
That of an elder cannot enter a gourd.

Within the family, as well as in public life, the roles of elder and child are distinctly separate. It is an elder's duty to head his or her family or community. Elders must provide for this group's material needs, guide it spiritually and ethically, and must also always appear serious and responsible. In return, elders have the right to be treated respectfully by everybody. They are always first to be served at the table. Their meals are presented reverently, and the most succulent part of any dish is kept for them. At the other end of the scale, children have no decision-making authority. A child's main duty is to do the bidding of any adults in the group, and to assist them with whatever tasks they can. The primary role of children is thus to obey and to learn. Aside from their duties, children have the right to be well fed and cared for, as well as the right to play and to be happy.

The social positions ascribed to the elder and the child are derived from traditional Yoruba concepts. The elder is considered to be more experienced, nearer to the ancestors and therefore wiser; while the child is perceived as naïve, fickle, vulnerable, lacking in memory and thus unreliable. The elder represents qualities of strength and dependability, while the child is the symbol of weakness. Nonetheless, it must be noted that certain rites and immolations call for functions that only a child can perform, by virtue of the innocence attributed to childhood.

The proverb acknowledges this Yoruba perspective but warns that even the strongest and the wisest have their limits while the feeblest and the silliest still have something to offer. It is used mostly to explain that, as total self-sufficiency is impossible, we must not write-off or maltreat someone merely because we believe ourselves to be socially superior.

Omode gbon,
Agba gbon,
Ni a fi da Ile Ife.

The child is wise,
The elder is wise.
On this principle, Ile Ife was created.

Ile-Ife (from *Ilè n fe* meaning "the earth is expanding" is the mythical cradle of mankind and the spiritual capital of the Yoruba. Unlike Eden in the cosmogony of Judaism, Christianity and Islam, Ile-Ife is a real place. It is a town that lies in the western region of Nigeria, and is considered sacred and unique.

In this proverb Ile-Ife is used to symbolize Yoruba gods, myths, rites and beliefs, and indeed everything that constitutes Yoruba culture. The Yoruba are conscious that theirs is a complex, multifaceted heritage and, in order to conceive of it in all its complexity, one needs to cultivate a broad-minded, holistic approach which combines intuitive spirituality with analytical thought. In the proverb above, this capacity has been denominated wisdom.

The proverb appears to be paradoxical, given that children are not usually considered wise. The impact of the proverb relies on this apparent contradiction. It asserts that Yoruba culture has only developed through the collaboration of everybody in society, without discriminating against or excluding anyone.

Everyone has something to offer, and it would be injudicious to think otherwise. The proverb is also used humorously as an observation when someone unexpectedly makes a valuable contribution.

Ologbon ko te ara re n'ifa,
Omoran ko fi ara re joye,
Obe ti omu ke le gbe çku idi re.

No wise man can initiate himself into the Ifa cult,
No expert can confer nobility on himself,
The sharpest of knives cannot carve its own handle.

Ifa is a system of divination said to have been handed down by the god *Òrúnmìlà*. The supreme members of the *Ifa* cult are the *babalawo,* meaning "father of secrets". The *babalawo* constitute one of the most learned classes in traditional society, and perform many social roles. They act as seers, healers and priests who officiate over a number of rites. In addition, they are society's historians, philosophers and psychiatrists. The centrality of the supernatural in the Yoruba outlook on life confers on the *babalawo* a place of honour in society: most people treat him with deference, if not awe. To be initiated as a *babalawo* – and thus a full member of the *Ifa* cult – requires years of study. During this time, the initiate must undergo practical preparations and overcome challenges, after which he may finally undertake the rites by which the title of *babalawo* is conferred by other senior members of the cult.

Among the nobility too, advancement may be conferred by others. The nobles of the Yoruba kingdoms act mainly as advisers and ministers to the monarch. Each noble is considered an expert and is placed in charge of a specific sector of the kingdom's affairs. In addition to the hereditary nobility, there are situations whereby nobility can be conferred upon a subject, in recognition of his or her outstanding contribution to society. Nevertheless all titles, even ones that are nominally hereditary, must be conferred by the king after consultation with a council of other nobles.

This proverb is used to explain the necessity for collaboration in certain aspects of life. It refers to circumstances where one cannot obtain the desired goals unaided, even though one might seem to be entitled to them by birthright or merit.

Awo ni igbe awo ni igbónwo,
bi awo ko ba gbe awo ni igbonwo,
Awo a te.

It is the cult member who holds the elbow of
his fellow member,
If he fails to hold the elbow of his fellow
member,
The cult will be sullied.

Awo is the secret of life and its mystery. It is the
enigmatic language used by the gods and the
ancestors to explain the codes that govern the world
to those few people who possess the wisdom to
comprehend and explain it. Events and hypotheses –
be they human or divine – which cannot easily be
approached or explained are perceived as *awo* and
are preserved and treated with considerable care.

The initiated fellows of many cults refer to
themselves, and are considered, as *awo* to
emphasize that it is they who are versed in mystery,
while the other members of the society (the
uninitiated) are the *ògberi*. The latter are regarded
as ignorant and lack the knowledge, privilege, power
and responsibilities exclusive to the former. During
the rites of *awo*, one of the many symbolic gestures
performed is that of holding each other's elbows. One
of the things the act signifies is unity.

Amongst the Yoruba it is well known that one is
placed on a particular spiritual or material plane

according to whether or not one is a member of a cult. Initiates are thus separated from the uninitiated not only during their lifetime but even after death. The initiated are considered – indeed often *accused* – of being part of a privileged sect. Cults are viewed by most people as guilds that use their influence to favour their members. Many people join these cults not so much out of spiritual conviction or a quest for mystery or knowledge, but rather to benefit from their presumed privileges and power.

Although initiated people are seen as powerful, their main strength lies in collaboration. In this proverb, the virtue of cooperation is extolled by demonstrating how the honour, respect, power and privileges that the cult confers on the initiated rely solely on the capacity of its members to sustain one another. Without this, all power and mystery would evaporate and the cult would be disgraced.

The saying is usually used to advise people to collaborate with and help other members of their community or family. It is also used to justify an intervention that favours a fellow group member, or the whole of the intervener's community or family.

Ajá ti o ni eni l'ehin a pa obo;
Eyi ti ko ni eni l'ehin a pa òfo;
Obo ti oba ni eni l'ehin le pa òtòtò enia.

**A dog with someone behind it can kill a
monkey;
The one without anybody behind it will kill
nothing;
And the monkey with someone behind it can
kill a whole man.**

This pithy saying is rated as being very handy for
extolling the value of collaboration and mutual
reliance and is used mainly to encourage people to
stand by each other. It is also used in such instances
as when someone wants to reassure a terrified
interlocutor or to recruit a new ally. Similarly, it is
often quoted by a speaker commenting upon the
achievement or attitude of someone who has
accomplished something he or she would not
normally have managed alone.

The first part of the adage is built on the famous
propensity of dogs to be more menacing and
aggressive in the presence of their owners. The dog
is credited as being the favourite animal of Ogun,
the god of iron and protector of hunters and artists.
This proverb reveals that the Yoruba consider dogs
to be less astute and weaker than monkeys.
Monkeys, in turn, are considered to be lower than
human beings.

It is worth noting here that this hierarchy is not in the slightest an evolutionary concept: there is nothing in the whole corpus of Yoruba perception that endorses Darwinian modes of thinking. Research indicates that an animal, or *eranko* to use the Yoruba word, is considered to be completely unconnected both in time and in metamorphosis to the human being. A human is viewed as an entirely separate entity, called *Èdá*, and regarded as the created being *par excellence*. In the Yoruba concept of life, to be considered or called *eranko* is not just to be considered uncivilized, insensitive or a beast; it actually means to be considered a non-being.

Abata takete,
Bi enipe ko ba odo tan.

The marsh stands aloof;
Acting as if it were not the river's kin.

Kinship amongst the Yoruba is far-reaching and the definition of membership loose. Suffice it to say that in many cases the sharing of the same roof is as good as blood relationship in establishing and expressing kinship. A common term used to indicate and describe members and membership of family is *ara ile*, a "household member". Some other elements that determine and explain the structure and concept of the Yoruba family include the widespread practice of polygamy, the inclination to place emphasis on a common ancestry and the recognition of acquired relationships (such as marriage and adoption) as a form of proper and formal relationship.

The generic approach used to qualify kinship reaches its pinnacle in spoken Yoruba, which has few terms to describe family members. For example, in the absence of words for sons and daughters, *omo* is used to convey "progenies". Similarly, there are no specific terms for brother, sister or cousin. Relationship within the family is described in terms of comparative age rather than by blood-links or gender. The two universal terms employed are *èbgón*, "the senior one", and *abùró*, "the junior one".

In this proverb the principle of kinship is reflected in the natural environment where sharing and proximity is present. The aqueous nature of both the marsh and the river as well as their being such near neighbours is sufficient to make them kinsmen. It is, therefore, an unwise attitude founded on ignorance for the marsh to consider itself unconnected to the water just because of its different state. This saying is usually used to condemn those who try to shirk their responsibilities towards people with whom they ought to be involved.

A ki ito ba' ni gbe,
Ki ma to oro ba'ni so.

**One cannot be fit enough to live with a person,
And not be fit enough to criticize that person**.

This is a straightforward affirmation that living together entails rights and duties for all parties involved and the need for give and take. It restates the importance amongst the Yoruba of sharing a roof. The proverb is often used as a preamble to thorny discussions or to reveal unpleasant views or information to a member of the community or family. In rare cases the proverb is also used to warn people that, when it comes to living together, the aura of exceptionality fades as normality prevails and weaknesses come to light.

MONEY

O bã kuru, o bã pari;
Gbèsè ko si, esín ko s;
Onigbèsè ni o le fi eni sesín.

You may be a dwarf, you may be bald;
Stay free of debt, and you'll be free from ridicule;
Only your creditor can humiliate you.

For a Yoruba, certain physical attributes such as height and their possible association with shame or humiliation are not merely aesthetic considerations, they also have an atavistic significance. In Yoruba cosmology, a human's physical appearance is never a random event but a chosen design of the gods.

Although it is not the universal way of interpreting deformity (*see* page 50), in this strand of Yoruba thought malformity or physical imperfections are perceived as a form of divine chastisement. Consequently, the deformed person and his or her close relatives tend to be viewed with shame.

Despite the importance of this concept, Yoruba thought does not hesitate to challenge this general principle here, asserting that only lack of money can truly expose someone to ridicule. This axiom is, of course, used to dissuade people from incurring debts.

Agba ko l'owó a ni ko gbon,
Olowo ni se bi oba l'oko.

He who is old and penniless is considered unwise,
It is the rich man who leads the settlement.

While most of a Yoruba's life is regulated by and expressed in symbols and beliefs, a Yoruba never loses sight of the importance of practical action. Knowledge and meditation are very important to the Yoruba way of life, but a Yoruba also considers money to be essential to get things done. Money, along with children and good health, are the three elements considered fundamental to human happiness.

Broadly, there are two kinds of Yoruba habitation: towns and settlements. The town, or *ilu*, is more populous, more established and has a king and a court. The settlement, referred to as *oko* or sometimes *abúle* , is, by contrast, a temporary rural settlement with neither a king nor a court.

The town acts as an important reference point in terms of identity. One of the distinctive features of the Yoruba is their tendency to maintain a home and live in the towns, rather than staying permanently in their settlements. The inclination to live in the *ilu* and to identify with it is largely due to the king's presence there. The king is regarded as the father and guide of his kingdom. As he is considered the aide to the gods and companion of the ancestors, he is treated with veneration. Kingship is based strictly on heritage but, as part of the process of choosing which of the eligible candidates should ascend to the throne, the gods are consulted through divination. The coronation of a monarch involves elaborate rites and ceremonies.

The settlement is primarily farmland. People work and camp there during the week but leave it at weekends to enjoy the various festivities in the town. Should the population grow and its inhabitants start to refer to it as their home and place of origin, then its status would change from that of *oko* or *abúle* to *ilu*. Due to its improvised and temporary nature, the settlement has neither a king nor a real palace with a court. Leadership here is based more on practical requirements than tradition or heritage. The leader tends to be the one who gets things done and so this role usually devolves to someone with sufficient wealth to provide for the community's needs, regardless of age or wisdom.

In this proverb the settlement therefore represents a practical milieu while the figure of the elderly man – normally someone who is considered wise and authoritative due to his age and experience – signifies that wisdom without the capacity to act is not only insufficient but may even be detrimental. Human beings respect those who can act; those who wish to be respected solely on account of their supposed knowledge risk being ridiculed.

A já' ni l'aiya bi ailowó lowo;
Ailowó lowo baba ijaiya.

It frightens like the lack of money;
And lack of money is the lord of all frights.

This is another proverb that reiterates the crucial role money plays in ensuring success in life. Here, in rhythmic cadences, we find the epitome of the idea that, at the end of the day, financial problems form the most serious predicament a person can face. A pocket full of money, however, provides a ready solution to most problems.

To comprehend fully the way this point is conceived by a Yoruba, it is worth bearing in mind some of the elements which underpin traditional thought. The Yoruba world view is nurtured in a kind of conceptual humus where not only day-to-day personal relationships but also the transcendental ones between man and the forces of nature depend on a monetary exchange. In the Yoruba religion money is needed to buy the material things people must offer the gods to appease them as well as for sacrifices. It is also common practice for people to pay the priests for the services they offer.

Agba ti nfo ni kã lailowó lowo,
Bi igba ti ako aja ngbo ni.

**The penniless elder who commands in the yard,
Is like a barking dog.**

In traditional settings, it is common practice for heads of families to direct family affairs from their courtyard. They sit there and receive visitors and relatives, discuss matters of importance and give orders. Those accused of breaking any of the various family rules – especially younger members – are summoned to the courtyard, where they are tried and sentenced in the elder's presence. Older relatives also meet with the elder in the yard to deliberate on family affairs and to allocate communal duties. In modern settings, most of these practices now take place in the living room.

In this proverb, the symbol of the penniless elder is revisited to demonstrate how having a title or experience is not enough to solve problems. A person must also have resources.

Owó ye ile; osi ko ye enia.
Osi ni ije: "Tani mo o?"
Ajé ni ije: "Mo ba o tan".

**Money befits the house, poverty does
not befit a man.
Poverty makes people say "Who knows you?"
Wealth makes people say "I am your kin".**

This maxim is constructed around what is professed
to be the most important theme in society, kinship.
The word *ile*, meaning "house", is also used to denote
the family. Kinship and the home are generally
recognized to be socially sacrosanct – things which
must come before all else in life. The word *ajé,* here
translated as "wealth", is also the name of the
goddess of wealth who is symbolized by money. This
saying reveals a prosaic reality where money and
kin are concerned.

Derived from a popular hymn invoking
prosperity, this saying may often be heard as well as
many variations on it. It is used mainly to comment
upon attitudes which appear to be dictated by the
influence of money. It is also used to comfort and
encourage someone who feels abandoned or
betrayed. In such cases the intent is to enlighten the
disappointed person as to the true nature of human
beings and to encourage him or her to concentrate on
work.

Bi owó ba tan lowo re,
Eni ti o fun l'owó lo mã koko bú è.

If you run out of money,
Your first insults will come from those to
whom you gave.

This axiom presupposes that when a person becomes rich or successful, he or she will suddenly be surrounded by a lot of people who declare themselves to be friends. Warning against such an effusion of friendship, the maxim not only underlines the opportunism probably motivating the new friends, it goes on to envisage, perhaps exaggeratedly, what will happen when the finances dry up. The friendship will turn to animosity when there is no more financial support.

ENVY

Aja ti o yo ki iba aiyo sere.

A sated dog does not play with a hungry one.

In this saying, the well-fed dog is perceived as at peace with itself while the hungry dog is still restless and dangerous. The intent is to point out that, due to these dissimilar states of minds, any slight irritation or misunderstanding might easily deteriorate into a confrontation. We can deduce then that from the Yoruba perspective a person's social position has a remarkable influence on his or her social conscience and actions.

The saying is used to warn people who are currently enjoying some form of success that to continue to mix with people who are striving to obtain a similar status is dangerous and that they must be conscious and careful of their differences. It is also frequently used to explain that a person who wants something cannot really love someone who already posses that thing, and *vice versa*.

Abiyamo ota agan,
Eni n nsise ota ole.

**To the childless person, a mother is an enemy,
To the loafer, an industrious man is a foe.**

A woman with children is considered blessed. Perhaps even more so than marriage, motherhood gives a woman a sense of fulfilment and social status, both within the family and society. Her motherhood is signalled clearly in everyday life. For example, a woman whose child is called Femi, is herself called neither by her own name nor by her husband's but instead *Ìyá Femi* or *Mamma Femi*, Femi's mother. Where a couple have no children, the first response of a Yoruba is that the couple cannot have children. No credence is given to the possibility that the couple may have chosen not to have children, or that they may be planning to do so in the future. People are most likely to blame the woman for childlessness, and one of the reasons most frequently used by a man justifying his polygamy is that his first wife was unable to have children.*

For a man, labour is perceived as the main source of material well-being and it therefore confers dignity on him. This saying draws upon the tendency of industrious people to be so wrapped up in their own endeavours that they have no time for loafers and wish to enjoy and celebrate their success.

This proverb shows us that envy is an inevitable and natural component of life. It is used mainly to warn people heading for success to be careful and prepare themselves to face the envy that their success will inevitably stir up in others. It is also used by those wishing to explain that their unfair treatment has its roots in envy.

---

* A man in Ibadan even went to the length of finding a precedent in the biblical story of Abraham, his childless wife, Sarah (then Sar'ai), and their slave, Hagar, who bore Abraham his first son.

Kòkoro ti o je efo jare èfó,
Iwonba ni eweko ndara mo.

The insect that devours the cabbage is justified,
There must be a limit to the beauty of a plant.

Cabbages are considered unique among vegetables because of their exotic beauty and the intensive nurturing they require during cultivation. Their peculiar status might also be attributable to the fact that they were originally imported into the lands of the Yoruba.

This proverb, a masterpiece of sarcasm, is used to comment ironically upon envy. As with most sayings on this theme, envy is viewed as an inevitable by-product of success.

Fi gògò sile fun odawe,
Fi aye sile fun onilara.

Leave the gògò for the leafcutter;
Let the envious one have its way.

The *gògò* is a long stick with a hoop at its end, used for plucking fruits from a tree. It is one of the tools used by the leafcutters, those who harvest and prune fruit trees. Here it acts as a metaphor for the frustrated envious person whose only response to life is to use aggression.

While most proverbs about envy simply consider it to be an inherent human characteristic, this proverb goes further. Beyond suggesting to the object of envy how best to cope with it, it positively advises that some concessions must be made and written off as tokens paid for success. We are warned against clashing with an envious person since they are likely to be seeking an aggressive confrontation. Where the envied person's success or reputation is on the line, the aggressor has nothing at stake. It would be a wiser strategy to make some concessions.

A ju won ko se wi l'ejo,
Ija ilara ko tan bòrò.

"We are superior to them," is no evidence in court,
Time does not settle a quarrel caused by envy.

This proverb is an even clearer warning to avoid entering into any form of dispute with people motivated by envy. Successful people are advised that avoidance is the best strategy to take.

The first line conveys that, although it may be obvious to us, and even to others, that the envious party started hostile actions solely motivated by envy, this cannot be proved. Therefore we cannot use their envy to justify any retaliatory measure we may take. The second line warns us that should hostilities provoked by envy begin, they will not subside easily because they will bring to light many other hidden grudges.

Eni fe arewa fe iyonu.

He who marries beauty marries trouble.

The Yoruba language reflects that in the Yoruba mentality there is usually no distinction between the objective and the subjective admiration that is a precursor to the desire to possess. The Yoruba consider it normal that someone who admires something beautiful should, and will, sooner or later try to take it for their own.

Contrary to what occurs in other cultural contexts, complimenting a husband on his wife's beauty is neither a common practice, nor one that is appreciated. It is more acceptable that someone praise the virtues, rather than the physical attributes of a woman, when in the presence of her husband. The most commendable qualities are normally her altruism and industry, being a wonderful hostess, a reliable partner, loving mother or a hard-working woman.

This saying warns us that the person who seeks to possess an object of value, or to achieve something praiseworthy, will not only be admired but is also likely to stir up envy and competition.

Bi a ba ni ki ara eni ma l'owo,
Ara ode ni iya'ni l'ofà.

If we wish our kin to be penniless,
An outsider shall be our pawnbroker.

This maxim offers an explicit denunciation of envy.
If, out of envy, we wish poverty on our own family or
friends and our wish be fulfilled, then one day we
will find ourselves at the mercy of a far less
charitable outsider when we ourselves are in need of
help.

Though envy is considered a morally deplorable
sentiment, its condemnation is not based on any
form of ethical principal. To discourage envy, Yoruba
thought relies on practical reasons and appeals to
self-interest.

MUTABILITY

Kokoro ni idi labalaba,
Eyin ni idi akuko.

It is a caterpillar that becomes a butterfly,
It is an egg that becomes a cock.

In this truism, morphology is used to explain that nature's ever-changing life cycles bring about transformations. Accordingly, a plain Jane may develop into tomorrow's beauty while a weakling may tomorrow be transformed into a strong man.

The proverb is normally used in such situations as when adults deal with children or the rich deal with the poor. The more powerful party is advised against exploiting their current, and perhaps temporary, position of strength. Interestingly, there are also cases in which people who have the upper hand today use the same saying to justify their aggression towards the feeble. Their attitude is to squash them now, before they have a chance to grow.

Bi oni ti ri ola ki iri be,
Ni mu babalawo d'ifa ororún.

What is today, shall not be tomorrow,
Thus the *babalawo* consults *ifa* every five days.

The *babalawo* (*see* page 17) is the embodiment of knowledge in traditional society. It is to him people look when they need to understand what is going on in the present, what the future holds, and how to intervene for favourable results. Having been prepared to respond to these demands, he draws upon his deep understanding of the history, mythology and ethics of his culture, and communicates with the forces of nature and the ancestors, through divination of the *ifa* oracle. A *babalawo* commonly consults the oracle at set intervals (every five days in this instance) in order to stay abreast of the state of the world.

In this saying, the image of the *babalawo* is used to illustrate the impermanence of everything in life. We are all subject to continuous change. The invitation here is never to become complacent about your position nor resigned to your lot but rather to remain on your toes, prepared at all times to face eventual change.

Ogun omode ki isere gba ogun odun.

Twenty children will not play together for twenty years.

This proverb originated in the era when the slave trade was booming and the infantile death rate was high. It was almost impossible then to see a large group of young children grow up into adulthood together. Their fate was sealed by separation. If they were not divided by early death then it would be by the slave traders' chains.

Today, some people prefer to interpret the saying as a truism which simply underlines that twenty children will not play together for twenty years because as they grow to become adults they will develop differing interests and preoccupations. Whatever the case may be, it is generally agreed that the overall message is a reminder that since everything in life alters we need to be ready to face these inevitable developments. It has, however, assumed a negative connotation, as people nowadays tend to use it to allude to the risks looming over situations which seem excessively idyllic, such as an apparently perfect relationship flaunted in full public view.

Bi o ti wu ki o ri, a kii rerin abirùn;
Boya ohun ti o se l'oni le se'eni l'ola.

For no reason must we laugh at the deformed;
What afflicts that person today may afflict us
tomorrow.

This proverb is very much influenced by the Yoruba
creation myth in which Obàtálá, the divine moulder
who made all men out of clay, is also the protector of
the deformed. In one of the creation myths Obàtálá,
whilst intoxicated, moulded some malformed people.
When he sobered up, he realized what he had done
and decided to take all deformed people under his
own personal protection, committing to avenge them
whenever they were maltreated. In this sense,
whoever mocks or mistreats a deformed person will
have to face the wrath of Obàtálá. It would be well
within Obàtálá's nature to take vengeance by
inflicting a disability on the wrongdoer or someone
in his family. (*See* page 27.)

This proverb is used to condemn the short-
sighted attitude of those who consider themselves to
be superior to those with disabilities and imperfect
bodies and therefore entitled to despise and maltreat
them. We should be very careful in judging others
and in criticizing their blemishes or weaknesses as
we may bring the same affliction on ourselves.

Sikasika gbagbe ajobe,
Adaniloro gbagbe ola.

The wicked one forgets kinship,
The tormentor disregards the morrow.

The themes of this maxim are time and the human tendency to focus only on the immediate circumstances or, rather, the human inability to grasp the complexity of situations in their entirety. The saying can be split into two separate but related parts.

In the first situation, we find the Yoruba appraisal of those people who act wickedly towards others. They do so because, in their narrow-mindedness, they forget that everyone − whether lovely or ugly, wealthy or poverty-stricken, mighty or weak − has a common origin and is a progeny of the same stock, that is Odùdúwà. Odùdúwà is the progenitor of the Yoruba people and they refer to themselves as *omo* Odùdúwà, "the children of Odùdúwà". According to the myths, Odùdúwà is not only a forefather but also the godhead through which Olorun, the God in heaven, created the world.

The second situation focuses on those who, because they find themselves in an advantageous position today, tend to oppress those who are weak, without considering the possibility of the wheel turning in the future.

This proverb is used to condemn those people who, because of their present privileged position, act without compassion towards the less privileged.

MASTERY

Ibi gbgboo ni iro adaba l'orùn.

For the dove everywhere is comfortable.

As in many other traditions, the dove is a symbol of peace for the Yoruba. This proverb simply means that in order to get on well with others in any kind of situation, one must first be at peace with oneself.

In practice, this dictum is used mainly to address those who attribute the cause of their uneasiness or failures to others, as well as those who tend to be too shy or scared to confront new or unfamiliar situations. It is also used by those who wish to assert their self-confidence to their audience.

Alagemo ni o bimo on na,
Aimõjó ku s'owo re.

The *Agemo* dancer says, "I've given birth to my child, It's up to him if he doesn't know how to dance".

This proverb is centered on the symbolism of the *Agemo* dance. Although *agemo* is often associated with the chameleon, here it refers to the deity, Agemo. The *Agemo* dance is the main feature of this deity's liturgy. Unusually, during these rites, women kneel down and cover their heads, while men must remain standing.

The *Agemo* dancer (the *alagemo*) performs the dance swathed in a woven cloth and embodies the deity for the duration of the ceremony. Due to the complex, spiralling nature of this performance, many years of training and practice is required and most *alagemos* start their training from infancy. There are often ceremonies in which child *alagemos* take the dais and dance. They, too, are clothed in weavings and emerge from the adult *alagemo*, symbolically representing their birth.

This adage suggests that someone's deeds and misdeeds are entirely and exclusively their own responsibility. The figure of the *alagemo* and child has been chosen to say that, once a parent has brought up a child, any fault or incapacity is then solely attributable to the child. Parents and guardians often use the saying to caution or rebuke wayward and irresponsible youngsters.

Bi inú ba ti ri ni obì nyan.

The kola nut reflects the mind [of the thrower].

It is a common traditional practice to seek the opinion of the gods and ancestors before undertaking important actions, whether they may be in public life (for example, before choosing and crowning a king or declaring war) or on private occasions (such as before choosing a spouse). One of the simplest and most popular methods for such consultation is that of casting kola nuts. These hard, red-brown nuts are split for the purpose into four equal parts. So that the response to a query is unambiguous, the pieces of kola nut are cast. If two of these nuts fall with their inside faces upwards, the answer is "Yes" otherwise it is "No".

The saying focuses on this sacred practice but strips it of all transcendental influences and ascribes all the power and responsibility for the outcome to the thrower's mind. *Inú* has here been translated as mind but the full meaning conveys the fount of someone's thought and measure of his or her humour and character.

It is one of the most discussed of Yoruba sayings. One of the more orthodox interpretations would be that the proverb seeks to warn us to be mindful of our conduct. An upright man may expect benevolent answers, while a treacherous person will stir up malevolent reactions from the gods.

Eni ti o rerin ko ni ibawi;
Ori eni ni ipe ki a rin eni.

The scorner is not to be blamed;
It is a man's *ori* that exposes him to mockery.

The Yoruba live in perpetual fear of being derided, and in any undertaking they place emphasis on safeguarding their honour and cutting a fine figure. When educating children, or even when advising adults, one of the principal deterrents used to discourage unpopular social behaviour is the prospect of being derided. It is well known that, moved by the fear of being laughed at, a Yoruba will go to any length to project an impressive self-image, especially on social occasions, and try to fulfil society's expectations.

Literally, *ori* would be a person's head but it is also his or her personal divinity, and the symbol and seat of their destiny. Here the *ori* is brought in as the most personal, individual and incisive component in someone's life. This maxim serves to demonstrate that in the event of failure, suffering or oppression, one should not search for the cause or solution in others but calmly and courageously look for it within oneself.

"Jo mi jo mi," òku ònroò ni iso'ni da.

[Saying] "Be like me, be like me," makes one a harsh master.

The purpose of this saying is to point out how useless and even counterproductive it is to attempt to shape somebody according to our wish or image. Its starting point is that each individual, right from birth, has a unique character and destiny. Above all, the figure of the harsh master represents the loathed and reviled person who thinks only of being obeyed and never cares about the nature, needs or desires of those who serve.

In theory, the phrase is used to remind parents that they should allow their children to follow their own path in life instead of insisting that they make choices (professional, religious or matrimonial) that reflect the tastes and convictions of the parents. If they do not, they run the risk of being hated by their children, in the way that slaves and servants hate cruel masters. In practice, it is often used by distraught guardians to explain that they cannot go beyond certain limits when trying to correct their ward's behaviour.

Òrisa ti ngbe ole ko si,
Apa eni ni igbe ni.

There is no god for the lazy,
A man's arms are his support.

According to Yoruba theology, each aspect of our life is under the tutelage of a specific divinity. Each one of us, whether aware of it or not, has a specific god assigned to protect us. Exactly which god is determined by factors such as a person's profession, heredity and the circumstances of their birth. In accordance with these beliefs, each time a person wants to undertake a task his first step is to solicit the appropriate divinity for guidance and protection.

This saying begins by acknowledging these mystical convictions but concludes with the assertion that a person is in control of their own destiny. Although people tend to place themselves in the hands of the gods, each individual must shape their own life with their own hands. There is no protector or miracle for lazy people, as only those who sow can reap.

This proverb is mostly used to spur people on to act for themselves and to take responsibility instead of waiting for miracles to happen or for outsiders to help them. It is also popular with those who wish to emphasize their self-reliance.

Agboju-le-ogun fi ara re fun osi ta.

He who relies on legacy is abandoning himself to misery.

This maxim can be taken literally. It becomes especially resonant within the Yoruba culture where inheritance plays a very important role in people's lives. In the public arena, most noble titles are hereditary, as are the duties and privileges of social life that accompany them. The same principle is applied in the private sphere.

In ancient society, a person could inherit not only material things such as houses, land and money, but also slaves and even wives. While the practice of inheriting people no longer exists, that of inheriting things is still very much alive and accounts for one of the most frequent causes of vicious family disputes. To make things potentially even more volatile is the fact that, in most cases, when a man dies the immediate family does not merely consist of a single wife and her children.

Generally, the saying is intended to dissuade people from relying on others and to count solely on themselves. It is very popular with parents and tutors who believe a child is not striving hard enough because he is banking on his parents' fortune.

Eru ki ipa osùkà,
Eleru ni eru npa.

**A pad does not bear the weight of a load,
It is the carrier who bears it.**

This axiom is based in the widespread practice of carrying loads on the head. A pad called an *osùkà,* made from a piece of cloth rolled into a ring shape, is placed between the head and the load to be carried. When people have a heavy load to carry, they often expend a great deal of effort looking for or preparing a carefully-made *osùkà*. Or, if the person complains about the weight of the load, a third person might offer to prepare an *osùkà* for them, as if having one would completely relieve the user of fatigue when transporting the object.

In this instance, the *osùkà* represents families, friends and assistants that act for us. The saying is used to remind us that, at the end of the day, each person is solely responsible for all his actions.

"Gbà mu" kò tan iba...

"Take and drink some of this," will not cure your fever.

To locate this message in a familiar situation, we imagine a sick person in bed receiving numerous visitors. Drawing on their own personal experience and knowledge, each visitor brings either some advice or some medicine for the invalid. The saying urges those who are unwell to see the doctor rather than rely on well-meaning advice since what is good for others may not be appropriate for them.

The purpose of this maxim is to encourage people to face things by themselves and to make their own discoveries rather than rely on others or on their recommendations. It is often used by people to justify actions or decisions based on a scepticism of others.

"Ng o se iyá," ko le jo iyá;
"Ng o se baba," ko le jo baba;
"Wo iso de mi," ko le jo oniso.

[She who says] "I will be your mother," can
never be a real mother;
[He who says] "I will be your father," can
never be a real father;
[To whom it is said] "Mind the stall for me in
my absence," will never be the real owner.

This truism is used to remind us that no matter how
capable or willing a person who wants to act for us
might be, such a person can never be as effective as
ourselves. There is nothing particularly dramatic
about the message but what is striking is the form
chosen to express its content. In the Yoruba culture
the bond that ties people to their mother and father
is sacred. Such a bond is the source of many of the
principles and practices which permeate the lives of
the Yoruba people.

Nevertheless, in the Yoruba culture, one does not
have to be related by blood to be considered a
person's father or mother – it is sufficient to be of the
same age as that person's parents. The brother or
friend of a father is called "father". In everyday life
a person's father or mother is normally the person
who acts as such. The Yoruba value this extended
parental concept, and it is sternly reinforced by
teaching children to adopt this attitude.

Nevertheless, the proverb reminds us that, in reality, family bonds prevail over and above existing social conventions.

PATIENCE

Èso èsò ni igbin ngba gun igi.

Slowly and cautiously is the way the snail climbs the tree.

This saying is popularly perceived as a eulogy to patience. Climbing trees is considered an arduous task reserved only for the fit and valiant. It is also used to symbolize achievement and conquest in life. Besides being known for its slowness, the snail is also thought to represent calmness. It is used as an antidote to vehemence and here it demonstrates that to accomplish feats and realize our desires, what we need is more patience and caution, rather than rage and impetus.

Although originally used to invite patience in general, today the phrase is directed mainly at motorists and young people. Interestingly, however, those who are accused of being sluggish also use it, to respond to their accusers.

Pipe ni yio pe,
Akololo yio pe baba.

It might take time, but in the end,
The stammerer will say *baba*.

More important than the contents of this adage are its phonetic elements and the grammatical structure of the Yoruba language. *Ba* is the first sound made by those who are learning to speak the Yoruba language, for example children, stammerers and foreigners. *Baba* means "father".

The stammerer is used here to represent a person who has difficulty in accomplishing a task. The stammerer says *ba*, pauses for breath, and then adds another *ba*, thus saying *baba* – later than others perhaps, but he or she says it nevertheless.

This proverb is supportive towards those who are anxious or who passing through a bad patch. It encourages them to be patient and not to despair because in time all problems will be resolved. It is also used to comment upon successful outcomes that have resulted from difficult or time-consuming undertakings.

Ibinu ko se nkan;
Suru ni baba ìwa.

Nothing is achieved through anger;
Patience is the father of virtue.

The first sentence condemns wrath, which is considered unproductive to anyone aiming to succeed in life. The second sums up the Yoruba concept of patience.

Ìwa, which is sometimes translated as "character" or "good character", is that quality which encompasses all the virtues which enhance a person's life and allow them to prevail in all their endeavours. It is greatly influenced by Yoruba mythology, in which *Ìwa* is presented as a woman and *Suru* (Patience), her father. The personification of these two concepts shows how impossible it is in Yoruba thought to become a virtuoso without having patience. *Suru* is the father of all virtues, and the father is necessary to beget the daughter.

Bi elehinkule ko sun,
À pe lehinkule rè titi,
Bi o ba pe, orun agbe onile lo.

If the owner of the back yard is not asleep,
One has to wait in his back yard,
In the end, he will eventually fall asleep.

As the back yard is normally the least guarded part of a typical Yoruba house, this is where intruders generally enter. In the scenario envisaged in this proverb, the invader or intruder symbolizes someone who wishes to accomplish a task, and the owner of the back yard represents a hurdle which must be overcome.* Whoever wants to obtain something worthwhile must know how to be patient. An intruder cannot but wait, otherwise they will be exposed to the risk of being caught and therefore the mission will fail. If, on the other hand, they wait, the right moment will come and the house owner will fall asleep.

---

* To avoid misunderstanding, the saying does not in any way condone any illegal act, such as burglary. On the contrary, proverbs condemn such deeds using a high dose of cynicism.

Eni ti ko ba kánju,
Yío je eran bi erin.

He who is not in haste,
Will eat meat as big as an elephant.

The elephant here stands not only for a dish that will fill a table but also a very difficult prey to capture. In chanting the praises of some warriors and leaders, Yoruba may call them "Hunters of Elephants" or "Conquerors of Elephants". Such an accolade is given to emphasize their valour and greatness, whether or not it is tested.

This particular axiom equates eating with the great feats a person has achieved or would like to achieve. Urging us to learn the value of patience, we are asked to reflect on the fact that the little pieces of meat a patient person eats every day will, in the end, add up to be as big as an elephant. The proverb is normally used to caution those who wish to obtain everything immediately or those who do not appreciate the little things they do achieve day by day.

Aja ti opa ikun l'oni le pa oya lola,
Nitorina ki a ma binu pa aja.

The dog that captures a squirrel today might
kill a hedgehog tomorrow,
Therefore we must not kill the dog in anger.

In the game market, squirrel is valued at ridiculously low prices whilst hedgehog is highly prized. Consequently, for the hunter, a dog that captures only squirrels is considered useless and expensive to maintain.

This saying harks back to a time when hunting with dogs was commonplace. It advises us to be patient at all times, never letting our decisions be based on the desperation of the moment, especially when our choices and actions are irreversible. The dictum is mostly used to exhort people to be tolerant and patient with those who are still to mature or who are new to a situation. It is based on a remarkable dose of optimism that is not particularly typical of the Yoruba.

Asese won ologbo ni ijiya,
Bi o ba pe titi a to eku pa je.

The suffering of the newly weaned kitten is only temporary,
Sooner or later he will be able to kill rats.

This proverb is used to raise the morale of those who are downhearted in their current position, or who are worried that they will not be able to cope with a new situation. People also use it to recommend patience to those who have to deal with the irksome blunders of an apprentice, reminding them that these will end as soon as the newcomer has adapted to his role.

Ki iku ma pa eni ti nda'ni l'oro;
Ki orìsà ma je ki nkan se eni ti nse'ni nika;
Bi o pe titi ori eni a da ni l'are.

May death not kill our tormentor;
And the gods protect those cruel to us;
Sooner or later our *ori* will bring us victory.

Ori is literally a person's head. The fuller meaning, however, also encompasses some complex and typical Yoruba concepts. It represents someone's personal godhead and his or her fate is held within it. The belief in destiny plays an important role in the corpus of Yoruba ethics and mentality. Nevertheless, it is universally accepted that destiny is not totally inflexible, and that life is not immune to changes. Forces of nature, prayers, sacrifices and a person's *Ìwa* (*see* page 69) can all change a person's destiny for better or worse.

In this saying, sarcasm is used to exalt patience. The image conjured up is of a person suffering some form of injustice, sabotage or oppression, and from this scenario we are offered a glimpse into beliefs like the unavoidable mutability of life, and faith in divine justice and the power of *ori* (*see* page 58). Armed with these beliefs, people use the saying to give heart to those who are being ill-treated. Rather than worry, they need only endure, because the moment of revival is sure to come and they will be able to look their oppressors in the face. People who are at the receiving end of oppression also use the saying to hint that they are not resigned to their fate, but are merely patiently planning their comeback.

REALISM

Eni ti ko ni owo ki ipe alakara.

A penniless man does not call the hawker of *akara*.

Akara is a general name for a delicacy. It is often used as a prefix to translate the various types of foreign cakes, bread and biscuits which are now abundant in the Yoruba diet. The original Yoruba *akara* now tends to be translated as "bean-cake" since one of the main ingredients is bean flour.

In Yoruba regions, it is very common to see hawkers carrying goods for sale on their head, searching for buyers. The procedure is rather like a drama, where everybody involved knows when and how to play their roles. The vendors arrive in a neighbourhood; they sing out their wares to announce their presence; members of the neighbourhood inform each other of the arrival of the hawkers; the interested buyers call them over; the vendors put down their wares; haggling ensues; and finally the purchase is made. There are instances, however, when some people (especially children) call the vendors and then disappear or pretend not to have called. In such instances, the hawker flies into a rage, frequently venting a squall of insults and curses on the perpetrator of the hoax.

This proverb is used to deter people from starting actions they have no means of carrying through.

Maku ko mo awo, o mbu opa,
Maku ko mo iwe, o nmōku l'odo,
Nigbawo ni Maku o ko ni ku.

Maku is not an initiate, yet he swears by the gods,
Maku cannot swim, yet he dives into rivers,
When will Maku not die?

For the Yoruba people names are not merely a matter of preference or aesthetics. Much importance is attached to a name because of the belief that the name given to a child will strongly influence his or her life in the future. Parents do not always have the opportunity to choose a name for their progeny, however, because there are children who bring prearranged names into the world with them. For example, the first-born of twins is called Taiwo, the second-born of twins is called Kehinde. A child born with matted hair is called Dada. If a mother dies in childbirth, the baby will be called Enitan, meaning "a person with a tale". Where parents *can* select the name of their child, they tend to opt for a name that will bring the child luck, expressing the parents' hopes. In this proverb the name Maku, literally meaning "do not die", is this kind of parental hope taken to its very limits. In practice, however, Maku is not used as a name by the Yoruba.

Only those who enjoy the confidence of the gods are authorised to act on their behalf. In this way, only devotees of a particular divinity may promise or swear by the name of that divinity, since only these people know and observe the required commandments. Outsiders who transgress this are considered usurpers who risk the wrath of the gods, which may be manifested in random minor mishaps, or even fatal accidents. In this cautionary saying, Maku symbolises a person who, by virtue of the protection bestowed on him by his or her name, loses sight of reality and feels invulnerable.

Bi owo eni ko ba êku ida,
A ki ibêre iku ti o pa baba eni.

**If the hilt of the sword is not firmly held in a
man's hand,**
**He should not challenge the death which
killed his father.**

This proverb reminds us of the need to be conscious
of reality before undertaking any action, no matter
how important to us that action may be. To prove its
point, the proverb calls into play two very cherished
elements: the paternal figure, for whom
unconditional love and respect is reserved; and
vengeance, the measure of a man's honour and
generally regarded as a just or even sacred motive.

It is thus used to warn people to be aware of their
limitations before issuing or accepting a challenge.
It can, however, also be used by someone who wants
his audience to understand that he knows the
appropriate course of action and will carry this out
when the right time comes.

Arisa ina,
Akotagiri ejo,
Agba ti ori ejo ti ko sa, ara iku ni nya.

Who sees fire flees,
Who meets the snake recoils,
The elder who sees the snake and does not run
simply yearns for death.

Fires and snakes both cause panic wherever they appear. Elders, by virtue of their age, command and receive respect in any Yoruba community. This adage juxtaposes the figures of the snake and the elder as a reminder that we all have to bow to reality, and that there are moments when it is unwise to want to prove our rights or status or, worse still, to remain anchored to past glories.

This proverb is mostly used to reprimand people in a position of authority (usually elders) who, in the name of tradition, refuse to acknowledge the supremacy of a new, overwhelming force. Not surprisingly, it is very popular with young people who use it menacingly to warn elders of their strength. It is, however, also used by people who aim to prove that they are neither cowards nor quitters, but merely realists when faced with a danger they have no means of overcoming.

Eni ti nwale ni nsìkú,
Eni nsunkún npariwo.

Only the digger buries the dead,
The weeper simply makes noise.

The Yoruba consciously place great significance on formalities in all their activities. Funerals, marriages and the naming ceremony at birth are the three most socially inclusive, public ceremonies amongst the Yoruba. This truism praises supremacy of action over form using the example of a funeral.

To grasp this saying fully, it is important to understand that the Yoruba language has no separate term to differentiate the physical act of burying the dead from all the other rites performed during a funeral ceremony which, in some cases, lasts for days. Furthermore, weeping during a funeral is not only an emotional response caused by sadness or a sense of loss. It is also necessary behaviour, performed especially by wives and daughters, which elevates the ceremony into a proper funeral. A Yoruba is likely to greet with feelings of astonishment and indignation any funeral devoid of the respectable dose of tears and wailing.

Fi omu fun omo,
Fi omo fun omo,
Bi omo ba ti mu omu ko buse?

Give the breast to the baby,
Give the baby to the breast,
If the child sucks the breast, is that not the
end of the matter?

This proverb is used in response to those who tend to
dwell on a point of form rather than focus on the
substance of the subject matter. Those who wish to
avoid having a debate about the right course of
action, however, also use it to justify their non-
compliance with established rules. In this sense,
they are saying that it does not matter if you flaunt
the rules as long as the outcome is the desired one.

Bi Olorun kò ba se'ni ni baba,
Ki a ma gbiyanju se bi àgbà.

If God does not make us a leader,
Then we should not try to be an elder.

The word *baba,* here translated as leader, literally means "father". In accordance with the Yoruba concept of power, a person may legitimately preside over any form of organisation, first and foremost when he is considered capable of being a father to that group. One of the decisive factors in attaining leadership is therefore the natural attribute of age.

The proverb deliberates on this widely held belief and ends up refuting it. In practice, objective elements such as age are not sufficient to guarantee that someone is fit enough to undertake certain roles or activities. By asserting that only God can makes us a leader, it underlines the fact that certain personal talents, such as charisma, understanding and economic means, are needed to lead.

The proverb is mostly used to condemn those who, though devoid of the necessary attributes, demand to assume a place of power and honour simply because of their age or gender. It is also used occasionally by people who would like to draw attention to the fact that they are aware of their own limits.

A ni ki a wa eni ti o l'èhin ki a fun l'omo,
Abuke bo s'ode.

We say, "We seek someone with something
behind to give our daughter to."
The hunchback steps forward.

In the Yoruba language, a socially and economically
well-off person is also described as someone who has
"something behind", a definition that also fits a
hunchback. It is a witty remark used to condemn
those who hold themselves in preposterously high
esteem and who would like to occupy positions they
are not fit for.

Adie nje agbado, o nmu omi,
O ni on ko ni ehin,
Èkérègbe ti o ni ehin nje okuta?

The fowl eats corn, it drinks water,
Yet it complains that it's toothless,
Does the goat that has teeth eat stone?

This proverb, with its unmistakable rural origin, is used everywhere today light-heartedly to reprimand those who moan about wanting something else, when in reality they have everything they need. It is also used to rib those who complain that other people have certain privileges, when in fact these privileges are relatively unimportant. In can also be heard used positively to encourage recognition of those who are physically or socially handicapped by praising what they have achieved in spite of their handicap.

"Ngo o wo o ka igbo",
Ehin re ni ifi lana.

[He who says] "I will drag you through the
thickest of forests,"
Will have to clear the path with his own back.

A person who, motivated by wrath or a desire for
vengeance, decides to inflict an unusual suffering on
another person must be prepared to taste some of
that suffering himself. This adage invites people to
take into consideration not only how right or
pressing such an action may be but also to assess its
probable cost.

Bi a ò ba ni ohun agba bi ewe l'a á ri.

Lack of an elder's qualities makes us appear youthful.

Elders, as already mentioned, are automatically considered wise, authoritative and worthy of respect, by virtue of their age. Youths, on the other hand, are paid scant or no regard. Their lack of experience means that they are considered fickle and incapable of forming an objective view of things. Their main role is to obey and to assist whoever may be older than themselves. The elderly are very conscious of the privileges society reserves for them and they do not fail to put forward their claims when the occasion warrants.

This axiom injects a note of reality, however, and warns us that if the elders are not conscious of their duties and do not posses the qualities they ought to posses, they will not be accorded the privileges that relate to their role. It uses the figures of the elder and the youth to show that even natural, well-defined positions can be inverted if one fails to keep a sense of reality.

Omo ko l'ayole,
Eni omo sin l'o bimo.

Having children is not in itself the cause of joy,
Only those buried by their children have
really given birth.

The birth of a child always brings immense joy to a
family and the celebration to mark this occasion is
normally a remarkable one. A person is only deemed
to have reached true adulthood once they have a
child to their name. A childless woman is considered
incapable, unlucky or even cursed, while those with
children are considered blessed.

One of the things Yoruba people most fervently
wish for themselves and their loved ones is to be
buried by their own children. The popular
expression *Omo ni o sin wa o* ("May we be buried by
our children") is both literal and symbolic because it
will only come to pass if the parents reach old age
and if the children themselves have grown to
adulthood and gained financial independence by the
time of their parents' death. Funerals are very
complex and expensive affairs. Where the deceased
has no children, or the children are too young, or
materially or mentally unable to cater for the
funeral, other members of the family must step in.
This is normally considered a sad end for anybody.

This dictum wants to remind us that nothing, not
even the biggest of all joys, will guarantee us

happiness and fulfilment by itself if we fail to guide it in the right direction. It is normally used to caution those who, out of love, tend to overindulge their children and who fail to give them the required discipline and training necessary to make them fit for the battles of life. Parents also use it to rebuke their children, when they perform below expectations.

Aide iku ni a nso àjà morun,
Bi iku ba de,
Àjà a sonu, agbe alàjà lo raurau.

The *àjà* on the neck continues to function
because death is not yet due,
When the moment of death arrives,
It will wipe out the *àjà* and sweep away its bearer.

An àjà is an amulet believed to possess the power to
protect from and defeat death. It is therefore worn
around the neck of those considered to be at risk,
such as the sick and the àbíku. The term àbíku can
literarily be translated as "born to die". It is used to
describe those children supposed to have come back
to the world after death and who are always on the
verge of dying again. One of the main characteristics
of an àbíku is to die on their own birthdays, their
naming ceremonies, or during their own wedding
celebrations. They have the habit of dying and
returning to the same family.

The belief in *àjà* is *a* very powerful one, and this
saying seeks to tap into the strength of this
conviction, inviting people to take a firm grip on
reality. It is mainly used to urge people to take
responsibility rather than to wait for divine
intervention, and to act while they can.
Unsurprisingly, it is also popular with sceptics who
use it to cast doubts upon supernatural phenomenon
and beliefs.

PESSIMISM

Eniyan bi apãrò ni aiye fe.

The world loves a partridge-like person.

To say that somebody is like a partridge means that the person is dirty, poor and incapable of looking after themselves. Perhaps this person is so overwhelmed by problems that they have neither time nor means to care about appearances. The comparison with the partridge is based on its speckled body and the fact that its feathers often appear dirty.

This gloomy maxim assumes that, due to both the malicious nature of men (often expressed by envy) and the competitive nature of the world, people cannot but dislike whoever appears to be rising or devoid of distress. On the other hand, the sight of a miserable person will make people feel luckier and give them the chance to portray themselves as charitable. The saying is used to advise people who are, or who are about to become, successful to be wary of others.

Omo-araiye ko fe'ni foro;
Afi ori eni.

People do not want our prosperity;
Only our *ori* [wants it].

The literal translation for *omo-araiye* would be "children of the world" but the term is used to denote other people generally. *Ori* here is, above all, a person's guardian angel and personal divinity, besides being their cranium and the symbol of their destiny.

This saying gives an indication that Yoruba people are generally mistrustful of others, and do not like to talk about themselves nor especially about their future projects. There is a deep-rooted idea that, due to the competitive nature of human beings, people will never be happy about another's success; it stirs their envy and reveals their failures. The proverb tends to be used to admonish those who speak too much of their plans or flaunt their achievements.

Eni ti o ni êwà ko ni èwà,
Eni ti o l' êwà ko l'ewa.

The beautiful one is penniless,
The rich one is without beauty.

Èwa means "ten", and in ancient Yoruba society it was used to describe ten cowries. Here it is used symbolically to represent money as well as because it rhymes with the word *êwà* meaning "beauty".

The saying warns that one cannot have everything in life and that things should never be taken at their face value. Though many people will argue, this saying merely invites people to be realistic. It contains an unambiguous sample of the heavy pessimism and scepticism typical of the Yoruba vision of life according to which nothing can go completely well.

The saying is mainly used to put into perspective the optimism and enthusiasm of someone who believes they have found a perfect partner or solution.

Arire ba ni je agbon isale,
Bi a ku l'owuro a ya l'ale.

A good-time table companion is [like] a mandible,
If you die in the morning, it falls in the evening.

Here banqueting symbolizes people staying together when the going is good. The mandible, more than any other part of the body, is the most active while we eat. The second line refers to the fact that although, after death, the deceased person's jaw may stay shut initially, it is sure to drop open when rigor mortis sets in.

The proverb warns against the fragility of friendships which bloom in periods of prosperity and when one has something to offer others. It comments on the lack of loyalty innate in unions begun through mere convenience or common interests. It has a negative connotation and reflects a rather pessimistic and sceptical outlook. It is naturally very popular with people who think that those around them simply want something but also with those who wish to discourage someone from being too trusting.

Gbogbo l'odì, bi a l'owo odì;
Gbogbo l'odi, bi a à l'owo, odì.

**Everything brings malice, having money
causes malice;
Everything brings malice, lack of money
causes malice.**

The rhythm with which this saying is delivered in
the Yoruba language has made it very popular with
singers and many modern entertainers use it in
their performances. It demonstrates how impossible
it is to please people as it is part of human nature to
harbour hatred. Based on these assumptions, two
diametrically opposed scenarios are examined and
judgement is passed.

The first scenario is that well-to-do people will
naturally be envied. People will be accused of being
tight-fisted if they do not appear munificent yet, if
they appear to be so, they will be labelled a show-off
or accused of not doing enough.

The second scenario is that of poverty. Those who
are indigent will be tagged failures and others will
tend to avoid them through fear that they would
always require something from them. Should a poor
person not ask, he or she will be considered proud
and stubborn.

Etutu ko fe pòròpóró de inú,
Kinun l'omo-araiye ife'ni mo.

Ants do not really love the stalk of the corn,
The love people have for us is limited.

The analogy is drawn from the farm. To emphasize
its message, the proverb zooms in on the image of
the ants clinging to the corn. The ants' behaviour is
not due to love but instead to their need for food.
Their feeding, which is perceived as natural, is
equated with the need of human beings to protect
their own interests.

The saying is normally used to comment upon
treacheries, and warns people against placing their
trust in false friends. The message is not to trust the
people around you completely because, no matter
how devoted they may appear, they stick to you only
because they need something. It is also popular with
people who, perhaps out of jealousy, seek to discredit
their own friends' new friends or acquaintances.

Orule bo àjá mole,
Aso bo ese idi,
Awo fêre bo in*ú ko je ki a ri iku aseni.*

The roof covers the ceiling,
Clothes cover the obscene parts of the body,
The thin skin which conceals the bowels
prevents us from seeing the death planned by
the plotter.

The term *inú,* translated here as "bowel", is the key
word in this saying. It refers to the inside of someone
or something, being the most difficult part to view
and also being the seat of a person's innermost
thoughts and humour.

The proverb reminds us that, whatever we do and
wherever we are, people will always want to harm
us due to their malicious nature, and that such a
nature may be concealed but never changed or
uprooted, as it is an inherent part of man. It is
generally used to advise people not to trust anyone.

Èdá *nlu ilu ibaje,*
Elédà ni ko je ki o dun.

Men beat the drum of calamity,
Only God Almighty prevents it sounding.

Drums, song and dance occupy a central role in
Yoruba culture. Every occasion is announced and
marked with designated sound and dance. In
ancient times, drums were used to send codified
messages, and even today the talking drum is used
in festivals and by some modern performers. The
dundun, or "talking drum", is played with a
hammer-like stick, and is famous for producing
sounds that parallel spoken Yoruba. During many
rites the drum is still used to signal the various
steps of the ceremony. The drummer gives the cue
and the singer or the priest takes it and announces
the next stage.

In this saying, man and God are placed on two
opposing planes. Man who is èdá, "the created", is
presented as the drummer and, due to the
pessimistic and sceptical spirit infusing the proverb,
he by his very nature cannot but wish calamities on
others. The sounds that his drum emits, that is to
say his ways and actions, cause others misfortune.
On another plane, God is presented (not only in form
but also in substance) as *Elédà,* "the Creator". To the
Yoruba, God is the Supreme Being, the creator *par*
excellence and originator of all things and beings.

God, in this proverb, is acknowledged as having the power to defuse the evil typical of man. This is due partly to God's capacity to be righteous but more importantly, it is attributable to his greater might.

WORDS

Òrisa ko nika,
Ara ile êni ni irò 'ni kâkiri.

The gods are not wicked,
It is the members of our household who
spread our news.

The gods, normally blamed or thanked for the events that happen in our lives, are here exempted from all responsibility. We are informed that victims of wickedness have only themselves to blame because it was they who, by letting their plans be known to the evil-doers, exposed themselves to danger.

Saying that it is the members of our household who spread our news is a way of expressing that those we trust are the ones who know our plans. These people are the only ones who can reveal our plans and thoughts. The term *ara ile êni*, translated literally here as "members of our household", is a general term used to indicate one's family, friends and relatives.

This maxim invites people to be watchful of what they say to others. It is also used as a means of expressing annoyance by those who feel someone close to them has let slip a secret.

Ààbò òrò l'à à so fun omolùwàbi,
Tí o ba de inú rè a di odidi.

Half a word is enough for the gentleman,
It turns into a whole when it gets inside him.

The principal message of this saying is that those
who are capable of understanding do not need long
speeches. The idea may be found in many other
traditions where, in different tones, we find the
same message that a word is enough for the wise.

Current spoken Yoruba language is now highly
influenced by other languages, especially English.
People will often use this proverb substituting
omolùwàbi with the term "wise man," as if it were a
direct translation. While there is nothing deceptive
about this, it is worth noting that the term
omolùwàbi, strictly speaking, means a freeborn or
gentleman rather than a wise man. One of the main
features that characterizes an *omolùwàbi* is *ìwa*.
(See pages 69 and 74)

A ki iso pe a be eni kan lori loju omode,
lorun lorun ni ima wo oluware.

**We don't say we want to behead a person in
the presence of a child,
As he will not be able to take his eyes off the
person's neck.**

Juxtaposing the figure of a child, here used to
symbolize *naïveté* and candour, with a violent and
tragic event such as a beheading heightens the
impact of this proverb's message. Quite simply, it
warns us to be careful when divulging our plans to
others. We must learn to measure carefully the
calibre of our listener before discussing or revealing
serious and delicate matters to them. Like a child, a
person who cannot keep secrets or remain calm
when made aware of grave facts will arouse
suspicions by their actions.

This is a very common maxim, often used in its
literal sense to justify not mentioning certain things
in front of children. It is sometimes also used to
comment upon a situation where a child's
misbehaviour or lack of respect towards adults is
deemed to be due to what the parents or other adults
have said in the presence of the young ones.

Gbolohun kan ba oro je,
Gbolohun kan tun oro se.

A sentence may ruin a case,
A sentence may mend a case.

The Yoruba people are completely convinced that in judicial contentions as well as in domestic disputes the decisive element is dialectics. This proverb warns that we should always be very careful about the quantity and quality of the words we use because, regardless of facts and intentions, what ultimately decides our position in other people's perspective are the words we use and how we present them.

The proverb is usually used to caution and condemn those who, due to wrath or ignorance, tend to ignore society's norms and express themselves without paying due attention to ceremony.

Enu òfòrò ni ipa òfòrò,
Òfòrò bimo meji,
O ni ile o kun soso.

It is the chatterer's mouth that kills the chatterer,
The chatterer has two children,
And says his house overflows.

This saying cautions against verbosity and exaggeration. It is built on important convictions, such as the deep-rooted idea that others cannot help being envious of a lucky person. The consequence of this is that the envious will, if they can, try to harm the envied. Quite deliberately, the example chosen is that of having children, which is considered one of the pinnacles of blessing.

We must also note the idea that someone who knows the details of a person's life is the one who can harm him, not only materially but also through psychic means. A person's middle name or mother's first name may be vital information in the hands of a necromancer.

The proverb is an observation that whoever is harmed has only themselves to blame, because by talking too much they have given their enemies the means of destruction.

RESPECT

Bi omode ni aso to baba re,
Ko ni akisa to o.

Even if a child possesses as many new
garments as his father,
He still will not have as many tatters.

The intention of this proverb is to explain why a young person must respect his elders. The figures of father and child symbolize maturity and youth respectively. The tolerance and affection that every elder is morally bound to reserve for every young person, and the respect that the latter must have for the former, are given legitimacy by the idea that both are socially obligated to consider themselves as parent and child.

Here the rags of the elder represent the experience gained with age, whilst the new garments represent the successes and power that education and ingenuity can procure for a young person. The proverb is used mainly to admonish emerging youths not to look down on their seniors; although they may be less successful or educated, they still have the experience that money cannot buy and may therefore still have something to teach.

Bi ekòló ba juba ile,
Ile a lanu fun u.

If the worm renders homage to the earth,
The earth will open up for it.

Ijuba (from which the word *juba* is derived) means all
the acts and words used to defer to those deemed to
be superior by virtue of their age or social status. It
is a very diffused and open practice in Yoruba
societies and can easily be observed in both public
and private contexts. Children are required always to
be deferential to their parents and their parents'
peers; devotees to their deities; and even modern
entertainers still pay homage to pioneers in their
field, their own icons, to God, to the forces of nature
and to their elders at the beginning of their shows.

To the Yoruba, the earthworm has none of the
negative connotations that it is often burdened with
in other cultural contexts. In this proverb it is used to
illustrate and justify the importance of respect. It
explains the creature's habit of working its way into
damp soil as being attributable in an allegorical
sense to its ability to pay homage to the earth rather
than its need to feed on the soil.

It is used to teach that those who show respect
will obtain the favours and assistance they want
from both men and nature. There are also instances
where it is used to justify or comment ironically upon
opportunistic attitudes or obsequious behaviour.

Apepo l'ehin agba,
Se agba mbo wa kan a,
Ki awon omo wewe ri ohun pa.

Skinner of the elder's back,
Your old age is coming too,
And the youngsters will have where to skin.

Using herbs and their derivatives in the preparation of medicines is a very common Yoruba practice. The expert whose duty it is to identify and skin the bark of trees for medicinal purposes is the *apepo*. This axiom reasons that while barking trees might be useful or entertaining for humans, it is certainly not the case for the plants. Skinning the bark off an elder's back is used metaphorically here to mean insulting or maltreating an elder.

The saying is used to admonish the youths of today that it is in their interests not to maltreat their elders because when they become elders in their turn, the youths of tomorrow will maltreat them using the same justifications they use today.

Ibi ti agba pin si, ni omode mba a.

The arriving point of a youth is the stopping point of an elder.

As in the previous proverb, the appeal for respect towards the elderly is based on the idea that the youths of today will themselves become elders tomorrow.

Life is conceived of as a tiring journey in which they who started before the others and have already covered a long distance will, inevitably, reach the point where they lose their physical and mental vigour. Those who have just begun their journey and are still fresh and bubbly also have a long way to go. Therefore they should be tolerant and respectful, refraining from maltreating the elders because sooner or later they too will end up in the same position.

HONOUR

Alaso ala ki ilo iso elepo.

A person clad in white does not frequent the palm-oil stall.

The white robe stands for purity, and whoever wears it is also perceived as unadulterated and authoritative. Palm-oil is a red cooking oil, very common in Yoruba cuisine, and noted for staining whoever comes near it. Although there is no proof that palm-oil is associated with any form of evil or corruption, its stall has been used in this precept to represent a den of ill repute, while the person robed in white represents a respected member of society.

The saying is used to warn those who have, or desire to cultivate, a good name and want to continue to be seen as absolutely upright, that they cannot afford to mix with people who have bad reputations.

Eni ti egun ba gun l'ese ni nse lakalaka to alabe.

It is the person with a thorn in his foot that should hop to the one with the blade.

This maxim originates from the farming world where the incident described is very common. The person with a razor, representing someone with economic means or social influence, is the one who can help the afflicted or needy, or the person with the thorn in his or her foot.

On one hand, the maxim reminds us that if the person with the metaphorical blade runs unsolicited to help someone in need, others (including the beneficiary) may attribute such helpfulness to secret motives, irrespective of whether or not the behaviour was purely altruistic. On the other hand, if a person in need does not ask for help, potential rescuers may deduce that none is needed.

In practice, the saying is used predominantly in two instances. First, when those in need seek to assure a potential benefactor of their flexibility in terms of when and where they could receive help. Secondly, to urge people who are not being proactive to stand up and solicit assistance from others. There are also times when it is used to remind people directly of the need to abide by their roles, as any form of negligence or transgression will lead to misunderstanding.

"Gbà mi, gbà mi" ko ye àgbà,
Ki àgbà ma se ohun àlèmu.

**"Help me, have mercy," are not fitting words
for an elder,
An elder should not do things that will land
him in trouble.**

This maxim attempts to remind us that whoever wishes to be a person of honour cannot afford to act in a reckless way. It suggests that we should avoid finding ourselves in humiliating situations, such as having to ask for other people's favour and mercy.

To make its point, the elder is again the symbol of veneration and wisdom. No matter how unknown, wretched or minute elderly people might appear, courtesy demands that others treat them respectfully and look to them as a parent wherever they go; elders in return expect younger people to perceive them as more experienced in life and its mysteries.

The social conception of the role and figure of elderly people automatically make them likely candidates for leadership, and one of the first steps taken by those who want to be community leaders is to assume the air of an elder. They will adopt their dress, their manner of speech, and, where possible, they will buy titles. An elder or a "wannabe" elder who forgets to act in role and ends up in humiliating situations will jeopardize his or her status or ambition.

Aguntan ti o ba ba aja rin yio je imí.

The sheep that keeps the company of dogs will end up eating faeces.

Dogs are not considered as special animals nor are they treated with any form of respect. This is notwithstanding their timeless importance in such tasks as hunting and guarding properties, or their spiritual purposes, such as being a key presence during the celebration of Ògún, the god of iron and protector of hunters and warriors. One of the main reasons put forward for this lack of special status is the tendency dogs have to eat excrement. It used to be a regular practice for mothers to keep dogs mainly for eating the faeces of their babies.

In this saying, the sheep has been used to represent a person with a noble mind, devoid of any sort of reprehensible habit; while the dog is ignoble. It shows that even a naturally upright person will lose his uprightness if he mixes with dishonourable people, eventually becoming one of them, and that it is therefore necessary to mind one's company. It is also a very popular saying with those who try to justify social exclusion and prejudice.

"E jowo, e gba mi o," ko ye egúngun;
"Eran ni o nle mi bo," ko ye ode.

"Please help me," are not words worthy of an
egúngun;
"An animal is chasing me," are not words
worthy of a hunter.

Egúngun or *egún* are figures who perform in masquerades, representing the spirit of the dead visiting the world of the living. During the *Egúngun* festivals, towns are invaded by carnival parades that go from house to house praying for people and receiving gifts and money in return. The *Egúngun* are highly respected and feared, not only because they represent the spirit of departed ancestors but also because they and their entourage go about with canes to scare and even whip those considered hostile. Indeed, it is a widespread practice for adults to use the figure of the *Egúngun* to threaten children and it is very common to hear adults say things like, "if you don't eat I will call the *Egúngun*," or "If you don't come inside now the *Egúngun* will come and take you away". Even some adults flee when they see an *Egúngun* arrive.

In this axiom, both the *Egúngun* and the hunter – who should strike terror into animals – have been used to underline how ridiculous someone will appear if, when faced by difficulties, they do not act according to their role.

GLOSSARY

Àbíku	literally "born to die". It is said of children who are supposed to have come back after death to the mother and born again
Abúle	settlement, group of farm houses
Abùró	younger brother, sister or relative at large
Agemo	chameleon, also the name of a god
Àjà	*an* amulet believed to possess the power to protect from and defeat death
Ajé	goddess of wealth whose symbol is money
Akara	a fried delicacy made from bean flour. It is also used at large for biscuits, bread and cake
Alagemo	*Agemo* dancer
Apepo	expert whose duty it is to identify and skin the bark of trees for medicinal purposes is the *apepo*
Ara ile êni	members of one's household or family
Awo	device, mystery or one versed in mystery
Baba	father, master, leader
Babalawo	Ifa priest
Dada	name given to those with matted lock hair

Dundun	a drum
Èbgón	older or senior one
Eda	human being , creature, creation
Egún or egúngun	maskers
Eléda	Creator, God, the Supreme being
Enitan	literally "a person with a tale" name given to child to child whose mother died during birth
Eranko	beast
Éwá	ten
Ewà	beauty
Gògò	a long stick with a hoop at its end, used for plucking fruits from a tree
Ifa	a system of divination said to have been handed down by the god Orunmila; it is also Orunmila's name
Ijuba	act of acknowledging and paying respect
Ilé	house
Ile-Ife	a town in the west of Nigeria; it is the mythical cradle of mankind and spiritual capital of the Yoruba
Ilu	town
Inú	stomach; matrix of ideas and feelings
Ìwa	a person's character
Ìyá	mother
Kehinde	name given to the second-born of twins

Kola nuts	bitter caffeine-containing chestnut-sized seed of a kola tree
Maku	literally "Don't die"
Odùdúwà	progenitor of the Yoruba nation
Obàtálá	deity , the myths accredit him of moulding human beings from clay
Ògberi	an uninitiated or ignorant person
Ògún	god of iron, protector of artists and hunters
Õgùn	medicine, poison, spell
Oko	farm, plantation or settlement
Olorun	literally "Lord of heaven"; the Supreme Being, God
Omo	child, follower, servant
Omolùwàbi	free born, lady or gentleman, fine fellow
Ori	head, destiny, personal god head
Òrisa	deity
Òrúnmìlà	name of the god of divination; it literally means "only heaven know those who shall prosper"
Osùkà	pad for the head for carrying load
Òwe	proverb
Palm wine	alcoholic drink
Taiwo	name given to the first-born of twins
Suru	patience

FURTHER READING

There are many useful introductory books about Yoruba people and their culture; the following are some significant works most of which have stood the test of time.

Abimbola, W.
1977   Ifa Divination Poetry,
        New York, Nok Publishers Ltd.
Awolalu, J. O
1981   Yoruba Beliefs and Sacrificial Rites London,
        Longman Group Ltd.
Beier, U
1980   Yoruba Myths Cambridge,
        Cambridge University Press.
Eades, J. S
1980   The Yoruba Today,
        Cambridge, Cambridge University Press.
Fadipe, N.A
1970   The Sociology of the Yoruba Ibadan,
        Ibadan University Press.
Idowu, E. B.
1963   Olodumare: God in Yoruba Belief,
        London Longmans
Johnson, J.
1956   The History of the Yorubas,
        Lagos CMS.
Lloyd, P. C
1962   Yoruba Land Law,
        London, Oxford University Press.
Odudoye, M.
1972   Yoruba Names: their structure and meanings,
        Ibadan Daystar Press.
Smith, R.
1976   Kingdoms of the Yoruba,
        London, Methuen & Co Ltd.

INDEX